Fiddle Time Sprinters
Piano accompaniment book

Kathy and David Blackwell

OXFORD
UNIVERSITY PRESS

OXFORD

UNIVERSITY PRESS

Great Clarendon Street, Oxford OX2 6DP,
United Kingdom

Oxford University Press is a department of the University of Oxford.
It furthers the University's objective of excellence in research, scholarship,
and education by publishing worldwide. Oxford is a registered trade mark of
Oxford University Press in the UK and in certain other countries

This collection © Oxford University Press 2003 and 2013

Unless marked otherwise, all pieces are by Kathy and David Blackwell and are
© Oxford University Press. All traditional and composed pieces are
arranged by Kathy and David Blackwell and are © Oxford University Press.
Unauthorized arrangement or photocopying of this copyright material is ILLEGAL.

Kathy and David Blackwell have asserted their right under the Copyright,
Designs and Patents Act, 1988, to be identified as the Composers of this Work.

Database right Oxford University Press (maker)

ISBN 978-0-19-339858-0

Cover illustration by Martin Remphry

Music and text origination by Katie Johnston
Printed in Great Britain on acid-free paper by
Caligraving Ltd, Thetford, Norfolk.

Contents

The unaccompanied rounds from the violin book are not included in this book.

1. Ready to rock

KB & DB

2. Clear skies

KB & DB

3. Ode to joy

(from Symphony No. 9)

Ludwig van Beethoven (1770–1827)

4. Song from the show

KB & DB

5. Starry night

KB & DB

6. Paris café

KB & DB

8. Jacob's dance

KB & DB

Nos. 7 and 8 are reversed to avoid a page turn.

7. Gaudete!

Medieval carol

9. Sprint finish

KB & DB

The violin part is written out in full.

10. Bolero

Spanish trad.

This piece can be played as a solo or duet with piano, or as an unaccompanied violin duet.
The violin parts are written out in full.

11. William Tell

G. A. Rossini (1792–1868)

12. Country gardens

English Morris Dance tune

13. You and me

KB & DB

14. The road to Donegal

KB & DB

15. Full circle

KB & DB

16. Thirsty work

KB & DB

Return to the chorus after each verse. The music is written out in full in the violin part.
The chorus and verse 1 can be played in semiquavers with spiccato bowing.

17. Farewell to Skye

KB & DB

18. Lady Katherine's pavane

KB & DB

The pavane was a slow, stately court dance popular in the 16th and 17th centuries.

19. Dance of the Sugar Plum Fairy

(from the Nutcracker ballet)

P. I. Tchaikovsky (1840–93)

20. Allegro in A

G. P. Telemann (1681–1767)

Try starting this piece with either a down or an up bow.

21. Still reeling: next page

22. Mexican fiesta

KB & DB

Nos. 21 and 22 are reversed to avoid a page turn.

21. Still reeling
(based on *Blair Atholl*, trad. Scottish reel)

arr. KB & DB

Add your own dynamics to this reel.

23. Show stopper

KB & DB

24. Spy movie

KB & DB

26. Hornpipe

(from the *Water Music*)

G. F. Handel (1685–1759)

Nos. 25 and 26 are reversed to avoid a page turn.

25. Largo

(from the *New World* Symphony)

Antonin Dvořák (1841–1904)

27. Hungarian folk dance

KB & DB

(2nd time **accelerando**)

44

28. Wild West

KB & DB

29. Midnight song

KB & DB

30. Wade in the water

Spiritual

31. Dominant gene

KB & DB

32. Chromatic cats

KB & DB

33. Show off!

KB & DB

34. Little lamb

The violin part is written out in full.

35. Habanera

(from *Carmen*)

Georges Bizet (1838–75)